THE MYSTERY OF MARY SURRATT

THE PLOT TO KILL PRESIDENT LINCOLN

THE MYSTERY OF MARY SURRATT

THE PLOT TO KILL PRESIDENT LINCOLN

by

REBECCA C. JONES

Tidewater Publishers
Centreville, Maryland

Library of Congress Cataloging-in-Publication Data

Jones, Rebecca C.
    The mystery of Mary Surratt : the plot to kill President Lincoln / Rebecca C. Jones.— 1st ed.
      p. cm.
    Includes bibliographical references and index.
    ISBN 0-87033-560-X (pbk.)
    1. Lincoln, Abraham, 1809-1865—Assassination—Juvenile literature. 2. Surratt,
    Mary E. (Mary Eugenia), 1820-1865—Juvenile literature. I. Title.
    E457.5.J78 2004
    973.7'092—dc22
                                        2004010276

Manufactured in the United States of America
First edition

Building 20

*I*t's hard to explain some of the things that have happened in and around Building 20 at Fort McNair in Washington, D.C.

One Army captain who used to live in Building 20 has told of trying to comfort his crying baby one night. Suddenly he felt a hand on his shoulder. The baby looked up and stopped crying.

Later, the captain went into the kitchen and thanked his wife for quieting their child. But she said she hadn't gone near the baby's room. The captain was puzzled: No one else was at home, he told *The Washingtonian* magazine, and "I definitely felt a hand on my shoulder."

Another captain has told of being awakened one night by the sound of someone moaning and weeping. "It was a female voice," he told *People* magazine, "and it was crying out, 'Oh, help me! Oh, help me!'" The captain rushed downstairs—where the cries seemed to be coming from—but no one was there.

Other former residents have told of heavy chairs being dragged across rooms, washing machines being turned around, and doors being locked from the inside—all while no one was home. Children have described a lady, dressed in black, who comforted them when they fell. Mothers have reported glimpsing a similar woman, checking on children who were sick.

Not everyone in Building 20 has had experience with the mysterious lady. After living there for several months, one resident said the only strange thing he'd noticed was the sound of water bubbling in the old building's pipes. Maybe that's what people were hearing, he said, when they thought they heard a woman crying.

But many people—especially people who know the history of Building 20—don't think old pipes can explain all of the strange things that have happened there. They are convinced that Building 20 is haunted by the ghost of a woman named Mary Surratt.

In the spring of 1865, Mary Surratt was probably the most hated woman in America. President Abraham Lincoln had just been murdered, and almost everyone blamed Mrs. Surratt.

No one suggested that Mrs. Surratt pulled the trigger on the gun that killed the President. The trigger was pulled by a handsome young actor named John Wilkes Booth. But the government accused Mrs. Surratt of helping Booth plan the murder. Mrs. Surratt insisted she was innocent, but she was sentenced to death after a trial that was held at the Old Arsenal Penitentiary—in what is now Building 20.

Ever since her death, Americans have argued about Mary Surratt. Many people are convinced she was an innocent woman, wrongly accused and unfairly punished. Others believe she knew—maybe even helped plan—every detail of the plot to kill President Lincoln.

What is the truth?

A Maryland Mother

For most of her life, Mary Surratt was an ordinary woman who did ordinary things. She took care of her children, worked hard, went to church, argued with her husband, and worried about money. She even looked ordinary, with her brown hair parted in the middle and pulled back into a bun. If she had lived in ordinary times, it's unlikely that anyone outside Prince George's County, Maryland, ever would have heard of Mary Surratt.

But the 1860s were not ordinary times. A bloody civil war was dividing Americans. Northerners were fighting Southerners, and those who lived in between—in border states like Maryland—were choosing sides.

The Surratt (pronounced sir-RAT) family chose the South. Mary, her husband John, and their three children—Isaac, Anna,

Mary Surratt. *Courtesy Surratt House Museum.*

Maryland in the Civil War

The Civil War was the bloodiest war in the history of the United States. It began after eleven Southern states broke away from the Union to form a new country—the Confederate States of America—where they could make their own laws. The fighting lasted four years and killed almost 600,000 Americans—more Americans than have died in all other wars combined.

Abraham Lincoln, president of the United States at the time, insisted the purpose of the war was to preserve the Union. But many Northerners thought, or hoped, the real purpose was to abolish slavery. All the Confederate states allowed slavery.

Maryland also allowed slavery, and many Marylanders wanted their state to join the Confederacy. (Others, especially in western Maryland, wanted to stay in the Union.) In 1861, when it looked like the Maryland legislature would vote to leave the Union, President Lincoln sent troops to the state's capital in Annapolis. Soldiers arrested many lawmakers before they could vote.

The president's actions in Maryland clearly were not legal. But President Lincoln felt he had to do these things to keep Maryland in the Union—and to keep the nation's capital in nearby Washington, D.C.

Many people in Maryland were furious with the way their rights had been trampled. They thought of themselves as Confederates trapped in a Union state. Many young men—including Mary Surratt's oldest son, Isaac—left their home state so they could fight for the Confederacy.

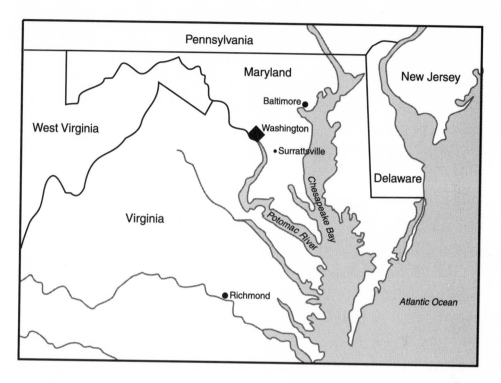

This map shows why President Lincoln thought it was so important to keep Maryland in the Union. Washington, D.C., is sandwiched between Maryland and Virginia, which had already left the Union. If Maryland left, too, the nation's capital would be in enemy territory.

and John Junior—lived just 10 miles from Maryland's border with the Southern state of Virginia. Like many Southerners, the Surratts owned slaves who worked in their house and on their farm.

There was certainly plenty of work to do. The Surratts were not rich, but they lived in a large house, with extra rooms for travelers who paid to stay overnight. They also ran a small tavern and a post office in their home. The Surratts simply could not imagine running everything by themselves without the help of slaves. And they resented Northerners who said slavery was evil.

Even in the midst of war, Mary Surratt liked to think of her home as a gracious, respectable place, and she often asked travelers and neighbors to join her in prayer services in her parlor. She called her home Surratt's Villa, and with the post office there, the area soon became known as Surrattsville.

But Surratt's Villa was not an ideal place, and the Surratts were not a happy family. Mary and her husband didn't get along.

John Surratt drank too much liquor, and Mary often told him so. He also ran up debts he couldn't pay, and Mary scolded him for that, too. Mr. Surratt said Mary was too bossy. The only time there was peace between them was when they were not speaking to each other. Sometimes they went nine or ten days in silence. Meanwhile Mr. Surratt continued to drink.

As her husband drank more, Mary prayed harder. She also poured out her problems to the priests at nearby St. Ignatius Church. In one letter, she told a priest that her husband was "spread out at his full length, beastly drunk in the bar room." She said he was drunk nearly every day, and she had no hopes of him ever getting better.

What worried her most, she said, were her children. She wanted to get them out of the house and away from their father.

Surratt's Villa. *Courtesy Surratt House Museum.*

When Isaac was fourteen, a priest found a job in Baltimore for him. Later, after Isaac left Maryland to join the Confederate army, priests found boarding schools for both Anna and young John. When Mary said she couldn't afford the tuition, the priests arranged for her children to attend the boarding schools for free.

With all of the children out of the house, Mr. Surratt drank even more. He was often so drunk that Mary had to put him to bed. Sometimes he passed out and couldn't be moved.

One night Mary couldn't get him up the stairs. She thought he was paralyzed, but his condition was even worse than she imagined. By the next morning, he was dead.

Mary did not know how to reach Isaac at the time, but John, who was then nineteen, quit college so he could help support the family.

John Surratt. *Courtesy Surratt House Museum.*

Young John took over his father's old job as postmaster of Surrattsville, but he didn't spend much time sorting mail. He was more interested in helping the Confederacy.

John never joined Isaac in the Confederate army, but he began carrying secret messages from people in the North to the Confederate capital in Richmond, Virginia. As these trips took more and more of John's time, Mary took over most of the mail work, even though her son officially remained the postmaster.

When the government figured out what John was up to, he lost his position as postmaster. Without the income from that job, Mary didn't see how her family could survive.

Then she remembered a house in Washington that her husband had bought more than ten years before. It was all paid for and right downtown, on H Street, just a few blocks from the new Ford's Theatre. She decided it was a fine location for a boardinghouse—a place where travelers and government workers would pay to stay.

At last, Mary had found a respectable way to support her family without worrying about a husband who drank too much or a son who took too many trips. Her life would surely be better now.

The House on H Street

$\mathcal{M}$ary Surratt had no trouble finding people who wanted to rent rooms in her boardinghouse. Washington was a busy city, and lots of people were looking for a place to stay. Two boarders even wanted to move in before Mary was ready to leave Surrattsville.

The first, a young lady named Honora Fitzpatrick, arrived at the house on H Street in October 1864. She and Mary's daughter, Anna, quickly became good friends and agreed to share a room. The second boarder was an old college friend of John's, Louis Weichmann. Lou paid $35 a month for his room and meals. He agreed to share his room with John whenever John was in Washington.

Mary still had to find someone to rent Surratt's Villa, so she left Anna in charge of the boardinghouse while she and John took

Mary Surratt's boardinghouse on H Street in Washington, D.C. The building still stands at 604 H Street Northwest. *Courtesy Surratt House Museum.*

care of things back in Maryland. Mary liked the idea of keeping her son away from Washington as long as possible because she worried that all of his talk about the Confederacy might get him in trouble in the Union's capital city.

As Christmas approached, Mary found a man who agreed to rent Surratt's Villa for $500 a year. Then she and John moved the last of their belongings into the house on H Street. John stayed at the house only a few days before he returned to his old job of carrying secret messages for the Confederates.

Mary put advertisements in a local newspaper, and the boardinghouse was soon full. A family of four rented one of the rooms, and another room was rented to a ten-year-old girl, Mary Apollonia Dean, who needed a place to stay while she attended school in Washington.

After so many years in the country, Mrs. Surratt enjoyed city life. Instead of asking travelers to join her in prayer meetings in her parlor, she could walk around the corner to St. Patrick's Catholic Church. She often went there to thank God for giving her a quiet, respectable way to support her family. She also prayed for the safety of her sons in the final weeks of the Civil War.

The war had dragged on for four years, but now the Confederates knew they were losing. People knew it was only a matter of time before the Confederate capital in Richmond would fall into Union hands. Then all would be lost, and the war would be over.

Now more than ever, Southerners needed a safe house in Washington—a place where they could rage about the Union or plan their futures, without worrying about who might be listening. With John still running secret messages to Richmond, his Confederate friends knew they would be welcome—and safe—at the Surratt boardinghouse on H Street.

Mary was proud of the fact that John's friends liked to come to her home. She was especially proud of her son's friendship with a famous actor named John Wilkes Booth.

Booth, who liked to be called Wilkes, came from a family of actors. His older brother, Edwin, was the most famous actor in America. Both men had grown up in Maryland, but Edwin was a strong Union man who supported President Lincoln, while Booth was a strong Confederate man who hated Lincoln. The Civil War split many families that way.

Anna and Honora thought John Wilkes Booth was the most handsome man they had ever met. He had dark curly hair, brown eyes, and a thick mustache. Local shops sold his picture, and the young women bought one.

Mrs. Surratt liked Booth, too. He was a charming young man, and he visited her house often, even when her son was away on one of his trips. She and Booth often went into a separate room where they could speak privately. Nobody knows what they said.

Mary did not like all of her son's friends. One of them, George Atzerodt, rented a room at her boardinghouse for a few days. He

John Wilkes Booth. *Courtesy Surratt House Museum.*

wanted to stay longer, but Mary told him to leave after she found several bottles of liquor in his room. She was never again going to put up with a drunken man in her home.

Booth was a heavy drinker, too, but he evidently did not drink in Mrs. Surratt's presence. He was always welcome at her house.

When John Surratt returned from his trips, Booth visited the house on H Street even more often. They talked for hours about what they could do to help the Confederacy in its dying days. They both knew the South was losing the war because it was running out of soldiers. So many Confederate soldiers had been captured or killed that the South was now forced to send old men and young boys into battle. Soon the South would have no soldiers capable of fighting.

Both men knew the Union held thousands of captured Confederate soldiers in prison camps. If the Union would release those prisoners, they could go back to fighting for the South.

But what would make the Union release its prisoners?

Booth had an idea. He wanted to capture President Lincoln, take him to Virginia, and offer to return him only if Confederate prisoners were released. He knew it wouldn't be easy to capture the president. Abraham Lincoln had received hundreds of death threats, and guards followed him everywhere.

But Booth and Surratt were sure lots of people in Maryland would help hide anyone who had captured the president. All they needed to do was get the president out of Washington. Among their Confederate friends, they knew of at least five men who would help:

• Lewis Powell, a large, muscular man who once had served as a Confederate ranger. He had a terrible temper, and he used a lot of different names. Sometimes he posed as a Baptist minister named Reverend Wood, and sometimes he called himself Lewis Paine (or Payne).

• David Herold, the only son in a family with eight girls. Davy grew up in Maryland, but worked for a Washington, D.C., pharmacy. He once delivered a bottle of castor oil to the White House and personally handed it to President Lincoln.

• George Atzerodt, whose liquor bottles had caused Mary Surratt to kick him out of her boardinghouse. A former carriage-maker, he spent much of the Civil War rowing

Lewis Powell   David Herold   George Atzerodt

Samuel Arnold   Michael O'Laughlen

Confederates back and forth across the Potomac River between Maryland and Virginia.

• Samuel Arnold, Booth's childhood friend who lived in Baltimore. Arnold had enlisted in the Confederate army but was discharged for medical reasons.

• Michael O'Laughlen, another old Baltimore friend who had been a Confederate soldier.

All of these men had lived in Maryland, and they all hated Abraham Lincoln. When they heard about the idea of capturing the president, they agreed to help. They believed that seizing President Lincoln and exchanging him for Confederate prisoners of war would be a legitimate act of war.

The only question was how they would do it.

Capturing the President

*B*ooth wanted to capture Abraham Lincoln in a theater. The president liked to attend plays as a way of distracting himself from worries about the war, and Washington theaters always advertised when he was coming, in hopes of selling more tickets.

As a well-known actor, Booth had access to every theater in town. No one would try to stop the great John Wilkes Booth from entering a theater or even from approaching the president's box.

Sam Arnold and Michael O'Laughlen didn't like this plan. Theaters were crowded places, so there would be lots of witnesses. Why not capture the president somewhere more secluded, with fewer people watching?

But Booth liked the idea of an audience watching his performance. He wanted to leap upon the president in his box seat, handcuff him, and throw him onto the stage below. The other men could run onto the stage, catch the president, and hustle him to the alley behind the theater, where a carriage would be waiting to rush them all to southern Maryland. They would take a boat across the Potomac River into Virginia. Once there, the kidnappers would surely be welcomed as heroes of the Confederacy.

Booth bought guns for all of the men and started watching for announcements of theater performances the president would attend. In the meantime, he wanted the men to learn their way around the theater. So he rented the president's box at Ford's Theatre and arranged for John Surratt and Lewis Powell to sit there.

They took Honora Fitzpatrick and little Mary Apollonia Dean from the boardinghouse to see the play *Jane Shore*. While Honora and Apollonia enjoyed the show, John and Lewis checked how the theater was laid out.

After the show, the men met at a nearby restaurant. Sam Arnold and Michael O'Laughlen still didn't like the idea of staging the capture in a theater. What if something went wrong?

"Well, gentlemen," Booth said, "if the worse comes to the worst, I shall know what to do."

The others wondered what Booth meant. They knew he liked guns. Was he thinking about *killing* the president?

Several put on their hats and stood up to go. If Booth planned to do anything more than capture the president, they said they didn't want to be part of it.

Ford's Theatre in Washington, D.C. *Courtesy Surratt House Museum.*

Booth saw he had gone too far. He apologized by saying he had drunk too much champagne. He said he had another plan that involved capturing the president in another place.

The men sat down and listened. Booth told them President Lincoln occasionally rode alone in a carriage to a hospital outside Washington, where wounded soldiers were treated. Booth outlined a plan to hijack the carriage and drive it to the Surrattsville tavern, where they would switch carriages and whisk the president off to Virginia.

The men agreed to do it.

On the afternoon of March 17, most of the conspirators met at the Surratt boardinghouse. They got on their horses and, in a cloud of dust, galloped down H Street and out of town. Meanwhile, one conspirator, David Herold, took a carriage and an extra supply of weapons to wait at the Surrattsville tavern.

Nobody knows whether Mary Surratt knew where John and his friends were going or what they were planning to do. Several people at the boardinghouse later remembered that she was very nervous that afternoon. Lou Weichmann said she didn't eat any dinner, and she wept, "John is gone away, John is gone away."

Anna was nervous, too. She banged her knife on the dinner table and told Lou, "If anything were to happen to my brother John through his acquaintance with Booth, I would kill him." Booth might be a handsome and famous actor, but John was her brother, and she didn't want him to be hurt.

No one was hurt that day. The men waited in a grove of trees until they spotted an official-looking black carriage heading toward Campbell Hospital. Booth and Surratt rode up to the carriage, ready to grab the reins. Then they saw a stranger—not Abraham Lincoln—inside the carriage. The president evidently had changed his plans. (The men later learned the president had

Elizabeth Susanna Surratt, known as "Anna." *Courtesy Surratt House Museum.*

gone that day to a ceremony at the National Hotel—the very hotel where Booth was staying.)

Disappointed, the men rode away. Most of them went, separately, back to the Surratt boardinghouse on H Street, but not Michael O'Laughlen and Sam Arnold. They told Booth they were through with his schemes, and they returned to their homes in Baltimore.

John Surratt later said he quit the conspiracy that day, too. But some people don't believe he quit. They point to the fact that he went to Surrattsville the next day to tell David Herold what had happened. He took the weapons Herold had brought with him—several guns, a rope, and a monkey wrench—to the Surrattsville tavern and asked tavern keeper John Lloyd to hide them.

Lloyd said he couldn't do it. Union troops often searched homes in the area for weapons, and he didn't want to be caught with anything that would get him in trouble. John showed him a secret hiding place, above the dining room ceiling, that he remembered from his years of growing up in the house. They tucked the weapons into the hiding place, where no one would find them.

On March 25, John Surratt returned to Surrattsville with his mother and a pretty young Confederate spy named Nettie Slater. John and Nettie went on to Richmond together, but Mrs. Surratt returned to the boardinghouse on H Street, where she sent a

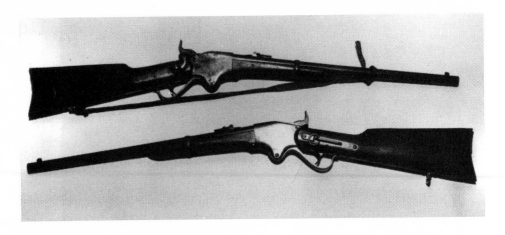

John Surratt put these Spencer rifles in a secret hiding place, above the dining room ceiling and below an upstairs bedroom floor, at his family's old Surrattsville home. *Courtesy Surratt House Museum.*

message to Booth, telling him she needed to see him right away. Booth went to the boardinghouse that afternoon, but no one knows what he and Mrs. Surratt talked about.

A week later, John and Nettie returned to Washington. He stopped at the boardinghouse to change clothes, and talked with his mother for a few minutes. John went out that evening to eat oysters with his old friend Lou Weichmann, but Lou returned to the boardinghouse by himself. He told Mrs. Surratt that John was spending the night in a hotel and would leave in the morning for Montreal.

Mary never saw her son again.

Favors

On April 10, 1865, Confederate General Robert E. Lee walked into a Virginia courthouse and surrendered. He admitted the Union had won, and he told his soldiers to go home.

All across the North, church bells rang and people celebrated. Southerners—and some people in border states like Maryland—wept. There would be a few more battles in other parts of the country, but most people knew the war was over. And so were any hopes for the Confederate States of America.

John Wilkes Booth wasn't ready to give up hope, but his plans were changing. He saw it was too late to hope the Union would release Confederate prisoners in exchange for a captured president. The only hope for the South now was to throw the

Union into such turmoil that the Confederate government would have a chance to regroup and rise again.

And the only way to cause that kind of turmoil in the Union, Booth was coming to realize, was to kill the president of the United States.

No one had ever killed a president before, but two presidents—William Henry Harrison and Zachary Taylor—had died in office. Their vice presidents had become presidents, and the government had continued running pretty much the way it had always run. So if Booth wanted to create havoc, he knew he needed to kill the vice president and maybe other government leaders as well. He also knew he couldn't kill everyone, all at once, by himself. He would need help.

Booth continued to come to Mary's home for private conversations. Sometimes she sent Lou Weichmann to the National Hotel, where Booth had a room, to ask him to come see her. He always did.

One evening after one of Booth's visits, Mary told Lou Weichmann that she had to go to Surrattsville the next day, and she asked him to go with her.

Lou did not see anything unusual about her request. Mary had a lot of reasons for making the 10-mile trip to Surrattsville. After all, she had lived in or near Surrattsville all of her life, and her mother, her brother, and her oldest friends still lived there. Besides, the Surrattsville tavern still belonged to her, and tavern keeper John Lloyd was still her tenant.

Lou Weichmann, who often said he thought of Mrs. Surratt as a second mother. *Courtesy Surratt House Museum.*

But the Surrattsville tavern was also the place where guns were hidden for the next attack on President Lincoln.

Mary told Lou that she was under pressure to pay off one of her husband's old debts. In order to do that, she had to collect money that a Surrattsville man owed her.

She sent Lou to ask Booth if they could borrow his buggy. Booth said he had sold it, but he gave Lou ten dollars to rent another carriage for the trip to Surrattsville.

Lou took the next day off from work so he could take Mary to Surrattsville. They left the boardinghouse around nine o'clock. As they crossed a bridge on the way to Surrattsville, they met John Lloyd driving his buggy in the opposite direction. Both stopped, and Mary asked Lloyd to get out of his buggy because she wanted to talk to him.

They spoke so quietly that Lou couldn't hear what they were saying, but Lloyd later said that Mrs. Surratt asked about the guns her son had hidden above the dining room ceiling at the Surrattsville tavern. Lloyd told her the weapons were still hidden because he was afraid Union soldiers might search his house. He said he was thinking about burying the guns. Mary told him not to do that.

"She told me to get them out ready," Lloyd later testified, "that they would be wanted soon."

That afternoon Mary saw the man who owed her money, but he said he couldn't pay, so there was no way she could pay off her husband's old debt. She and Lou returned to Washington that night.

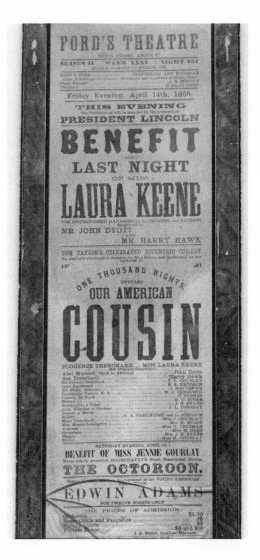

Hoping to draw more customers, theaters often advertised when President Lincoln planned to attend a performance. This playbill announced the president's plans to see *Our American Cousin. From the Joan L. Chaconas collection.*

Three days later, Mary and Lou got up early to attend Good Friday services at St. Patrick's Church. A few blocks away, Booth slept in and was the last person that day to eat breakfast at the National Hotel.

When he went to Ford's Theatre to pick up his mail, he heard that President Lincoln would be attending that evening's performance of *Our American Cousin*. This would be his chance to kill the president.

He quickly called a meeting of the conspirators who were still in Washington. He told them about his plan to shoot the president. And he told them other Union leaders must be killed as well.

When Booth told George Atzerodt to kill Vice President Andrew Johnson, Atzerodt said he wouldn't do it. He said he had agreed to *capture* the president, not *kill* the vice president. But Booth told him he was in too deep, and it was too late to back out now.

Booth also told Lewis Powell to kill Secretary of State William Seward. Powell didn't object, even when Booth told him Seward was in bed with a broken jaw after a carriage accident, so Powell would have to go to his house. Booth told David Herold to help Powell find the secretary of state's house.

All of the killings should be done around ten o'clock that night, Booth said. The killers should leave Washington immediately, so they could all meet at the Surrattsville tavern.

Lou Weichmann's office closed early that day so workers could attend Good Friday services. After the services, he returned to the boardinghouse, where Mary said she needed to go to Surrattsville again because she had received another pressing letter about her husband's debts. Would Lou go with her? And would he please go to the public stables and rent another horse and buggy? Lou agreed, and she gave him ten dollars to rent the horse and buggy.

As he was leaving the house, he met John Wilkes Booth. Booth had a package he wanted Mary to take to the Surrattsville tavern.

On the way to Surrattsville, Lou and Mary saw several soldiers standing alongside the road. Mary asked them whether they would stay there all night, and they told her they generally left around eight o'clock at night.

"I am glad to know that," she said.

Tavern keeper John Lloyd was not at the tavern when they arrived. So Mary gave Booth's package—which contained field glasses—to Lloyd's sister-in-law. She then asked Lou to write a letter to the man who owed her money. He puzzled over why Mrs. Surratt would make an hour's trip to Surrattsville and then send the man a letter rather than talking with him herself.

Lloyd arrived at the tavern late in the afternoon. He later said Mary showed him the package she had brought and told him to get out some whiskey and the guns her son had hidden.

Someone would be coming to the tavern that night to pick them up.

Mrs. Surratt then said she had to leave. The Navy Yard Bridge closed every night, and she did not want to be stuck on the Maryland side of the river. She said she had an appointment that night.

But Mary and Lou couldn't leave right away. When they went out to their buggy, they found one of its springs had come loose. Lloyd tied the spring in place with a piece of rope. With the buggy fixed, Mary and Lou returned to Washington in time for her appointment—and for one of the most dramatic nights in American history.

Bloody Night

*T*he evening started off quietly enough. A letter had arrived from John that day, and Anna read it aloud. The letter said John was in Montreal and liked the city very much.

Anna said she wasn't feeling well and went to bed. Mary and one of her boarders, Eliza Holohan, set out to attend another Good Friday service at St. Patrick's Church. They walked less than a block before a steady drizzle changed their minds. They returned to the boardinghouse and talked for a few minutes before Holohan went upstairs to the room she shared with her husband and two children.

Around nine o'clock, Mrs. Surratt's "appointment" arrived. Listening from his room upstairs, Lou thought it was John Wilkes Booth, but he wasn't sure. By ten o'clock, the man had

This is probably the last photograph of Abraham Lincoln, taken about a month before his death. *Courtesy Surratt House Museum.*

left, and everyone in the house but Mary Surratt had gone to bed.

A few blocks away, John Wilkes Booth was throwing back drinks in a tavern next door to Ford's Theatre. Another man recognized Booth and said, "You'll never be the actor your father was!"

"When I leave the stage," Booth told him, "I will be the most famous man in America."

Then he went to Ford's Theatre. He climbed the stairs to the balcony and walked down a narrow hallway to the presidential box. He had a dagger and a small gun—a derringer that could fire only one shot—in his pocket.

A guard was supposed to be standing outside the box, but President Lincoln had told the man to find a seat for himself in the audience so he could enjoy the play. (After watching the play for a few minutes, the guard got bored and went to the tavern next door.) So there was no one outside the president's box when Booth arrived.

He peeked through a hole in the door and saw President Lincoln sitting in a rocking chair next to his wife. Also in the president's box were the Lincolns' guests, Major Henry Rathbone and his fiancée, Clara Harris.

Booth waited for a few minutes and listened to the actors on the stage below. He knew the play—*Our American Cousin*—well, and he was waiting for a line that always filled the theater with

No photographer was present when John Wilkes Booth shot President Lincoln, of course, so magazine artists tried to re-create the scene. This sketch was published in *Harper's Weekly. Courtesy Library of Congress.*

laughter. When he heard it, he quietly stepped inside the door and aimed his gun at the back of the president's head.

The line—"*You sockdologizing old man trap!*"—might not sound funny today, but the audience in Ford's Theatre that night roared with laughter. When the audience heard a gunshot, some people thought it was part of the joke.

But it was no joke. President Lincoln slumped forward, and Booth rushed past Mrs. Lincoln. When Major Rathbone leapt forward to stop him, Booth stabbed him with the dagger.

Then he jumped to the stage, 11 feet below. As an actor, Booth had jumped even farther and landed safely before. But

After Booth landed on the stage, some people in the audience thought he shouted, *"Sic semper tyrannis!"* ("Thus always to tyrants!") Others thought he said something else or nothing at all. *Courtesy Lincoln Museum, Fort Wayne, Indiana. (Ref. 904)*

this time his spurs caught on the bunting that decorated the president's box, and he broke his leg when he landed on the stage.

But no broken leg was going to stop John Wilkes Booth. He quickly hobbled offstage and out the back door. He threw himself onto his horse and galloped away.

Some people in the audience thought the man leaping on stage was part of the play. Then Mrs. Lincoln screamed.

A young doctor in the audience ran to the president's box. When he found that President Lincoln had stopped breathing, the doctor moved his arms to get him breathing again. This maneuver worked, but it did not save the president. Abraham Lincoln never regained consciousness.

Other doctors arrived and agreed the president was too injured to travel even the few blocks to the White House. They carried him across the street to a boardinghouse, where they laid him in a bed that was too short for his long legs.

The other assassinations did not go as planned. George Atzerodt did not even try to kill Vice President Andrew Johnson. He just went to a hotel bar and got drunk.

Lewis Powell stabbed, but did not kill, Secretary of State William Seward and his sons. David Herold, who was supposed to help Powell find his way out of Washington, waited outside until one of Seward's servants came screaming out of the house. Frightened, Herold galloped away.

This *Harper's Weekly* woodcut shows Lewis Powell charging up the stairs to Secretary of State William Seward's bedroom. Seward's sons tried to block him, but Powell stabbed them and their father. *From the Joan L. Chaconas collection.*

When Powell stumbled out of the house and found Herold gone, he didn't know where to go. But he knew he had to hide.

Top government officials gathered at the boardinghouse where President Lincoln lay dying. When Secretary of War Edwin

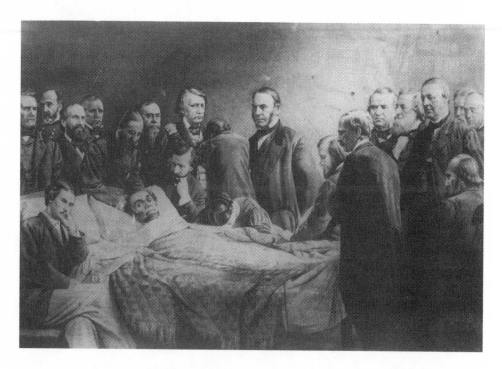

President Lincoln died in a small room that couldn't hold all of these people at once, but an artist drew this deathbed scene to show everyone who visited the president that night. His wife, Mary Todd Lincoln, weeps over the bed, and his son Robert Todd Lincoln sits in the lower left corner. Another son, twelve-year-old Tad, stayed at the White House. *Courtesy Lincoln Museum, Fort Wayne, Indiana. (Ref. 9A)*

Stanton heard that the secretary of state had been attacked as well, he figured the Confederates were making one last effort to destroy the Union. So Stanton ordered the arrest of anyone associated with John Wilkes Booth, who had been recognized by several people at Ford's Theatre.

The newspapers said soldiers rounded up hundreds of people in Washington that night, but Booth himself escaped. He crossed the East Branch of the Potomac River (now known as the Anacostia River) into Maryland and headed for the Surrattsville tavern.

His broken leg slowed him enough that David Herold caught up with Booth, and they arrived at the tavern together. They picked up the field glasses that Mrs. Surratt had left there that day, along with the weapons that she had said would be needed soon.

They then rode on to the home of a doctor—Samuel Mudd—who applied a splint to Booth's broken leg and let Booth sleep for a few hours.

After leaving Dr. Mudd's house, Booth and Herold hid in the Maryland woods for more than a week. Back in Washington, the frenzy to find them was leading police to Mrs. Surratt's boardinghouse on H Street.

Suspicions

*J*ust a few hours after the shooting at Ford's Theatre, the doorbell rang at Mrs. Surratt's boardinghouse.

Who would be calling in the middle of the night? Lou Weichmann got out of bed, pulled on some pants, and went to the door. "Who is there?" he called.

"Detectives," said a voice, "come to search the house for John Wilkes Booth and John Surratt."

"They are not here," Lou said.

"Let us in anyhow," the voice said. "We want to search the house."

Lou knocked on Mrs. Surratt's door and told her about the detectives.

"For God's sake," she said, "let them in. I expected the house to be searched."

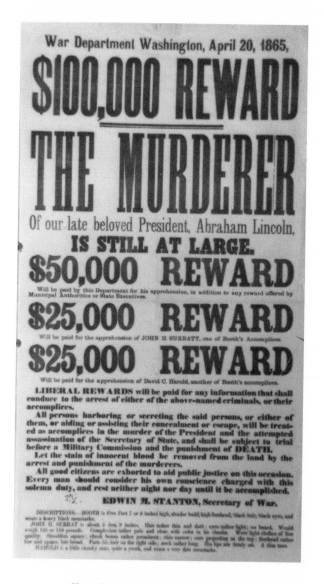

The U.S. Government offered rewards for the capture of John Wilkes Booth, John Surratt, and David Herold. The search for these men led detectives to Mrs. Surratt's boardinghouse. *Courtesy Surratt House Museum.*

After Lou unlocked the door, four detectives spread out to look through the house.

"Gentlemen, what is the matter?" he asked. "What does the searching of this house mean?"

The detectives told him about the shooting at Ford's Theatre and showed him a piece of black cloth with blood on it. "That is the blood of Abraham Lincoln," one detective said.

The detectives said John Wilkes Booth had shot President Lincoln, and they thought John Surratt was involved. They woke up everyone in the house and searched every room.

After the police left, everyone went back to bed, but it's hard to imagine that anyone slept. "My God! My God!" Lou later wrote. "What agony I endured until the morning light came through the windows!"

If the police suspected John Surratt of being part of a plot to kill Abraham Lincoln, how long would it be before they suspected Lou Weichmann, too? After all, he was John's closest friend and roommate, and he lived in a house that was obviously under suspicion.

Lou decided to tell the police everything he knew about John and his family. Immediately after breakfast, he went to the police station, even though he did not suspect Mary Surratt of any wrongdoing. "I did not suspect her any more than I suspected my own dear mother," he later wrote. But he never spent another night in the Surratt boardinghouse.

Another boarder, John Holohan, went to the police station, too. When he returned, he and his wife decided to take their two children and move out of the boardinghouse.

That left four women in the house: Mary Surratt, her daughter Anna, her niece Olivia Jenkins (who happened to be visiting), and Honora Fitzpatrick. Little Mary Apollonia Dean had gone home to spend Easter weekend with her parents.

Black-bordered newspapers reported the death of Abraham Lincoln. Some papers also reported that John Surratt had stabbed the secretary of state and his family. This was not true, but there was no denying the many times John Wilkes Booth had been at the boardinghouse. "I am afraid it will bring suspicion on all of us!" Anna said.

She was right. Over the next couple of days, police learned Booth and other major suspects—David Herold, Lewis Powell, George Atzerodt—often had been seen coming and going from the boardinghouse on H Street.

The newspapers reported hundreds of people were being arrested—everyone from the owner of Ford's Theatre to a man on the street who said he was glad Lincoln had died. So it probably wasn't a surprise when detectives returned to the boardinghouse Monday night and arrested everyone who still lived there.

Anna wept, but Mrs. Surratt quieted her and hurried upstairs to find warm clothing for everyone. When she returned to the

The front page of the *New York Herald* on the day President Lincoln died. *Courtesy Surratt House Museum.*

parlor, she asked the chief detective if she could kneel and pray for guidance. Certainly, he said.

As she prayed, the detectives heard footsteps approaching the front door. They hid while the doorbell rang and the door opened. A big man, dirty and disheveled, stepped inside. He was carrying a pickaxe.

When the man saw the detectives, he said, "I guess I have mistaken the house," and turned to leave. But one detective pulled a gun and demanded to know who the man was and what he wanted.

He said he was "a laboring man," hired by Mrs. Surratt to dig a gutter in the backyard. When the detective pointed out that it was almost eleven o'clock at night (hardly a good time for backyard digging), the man said he had come for instructions so he could start work in the morning.

The detective brought Mrs. Surratt into the narrow hallway, and asked if she knew the man who was wearing a shirtsleeve pulled down over his forehead. She looked at him in the dim light, then raised her right hand.

"Before God, sir," she said, "I do not know this man, and have never seen him, and I did not hire him to dig a gutter for me."

Later that night, when she was being questioned at the Old Capitol Prison, Mary said she was grateful that detectives were there when the man arrived with a pickaxe. If the women had been alone, she said, "I believe he would have murdered us every one."

Police took away the pickaxe and arrested the man. A few days later, they identified him as Lewis Paine—one of the names used regularly by Lewis Powell, the man who had stabbed Secretary Seward and his sons. Unable to find his way out of town without David Herold's help and worried that soldiers or police would find him, Powell had hidden in an empty cemetery vault for three days and three nights before hunger finally drove him to the Surratt boardinghouse.

Why didn't Mary Surratt recognize Powell? She undoubtedly knew him: He had visited her house many times, talked with her, and eaten with her family. So why did she say she didn't know him?

She later blamed her poor eyesight, his unkempt appearance that night, and the dim light in the narrow hallway. But the detectives didn't believe her. They believed she didn't want to admit any relationship with Powell because she knew it would connect her to the murder of Abraham Lincoln.

The detectives also didn't believe Mary Surratt when she said her son couldn't have been part of the bloody crimes in Washington. The last she knew, she said, he was on his way to Canada.

"No one on the round earth believes he went to Canada," an investigator told Mary.

"I believe it," she insisted.

She was probably telling the truth. Witnesses later said John Surratt was in Elmira, New York, on the night Lincoln was shot. After he heard about the shooting, he headed for Canada, where friends hid him.

But his mother had nowhere to hide.

The Old Capitol Prison

A carriage took the women from the boardinghouse to the Old Capitol Prison, a smelly old building that had once been used as the capitol of the United States but was now a warehouse for criminals. The women stayed in the Carroll Annex, in a small room equipped with old iron beds, a wooden table, and broken chairs.

The women's floor of the Carroll Annex was more crowded than normal. In addition to women arrested for crimes in Washington, it now held women who had attracted suspicion after the assassination.

Virginia Lomax, who later wrote a book about her experience in the Carroll Annex, said she was arrested simply because she had come from Baltimore—a suspicious place!—to visit her cousin in the Old Capitol Prison.

The Old Capitol Prison, across the street from the U.S. Capitol Building. The U.S. Supreme Court building now stands on this site. *From the Joan L. Chaconas collection.*

Lomax said another woman was arrested because she had not draped her house in the official black cloth that signified mourning for President Lincoln. Two young servants were arrested because they had laughed at a woman who wept over her washtub for President Lincoln. Another woman was arrested merely because she had been a friend of John Wilkes Booth.

Detectives questioned each of the prisoners, but they gave special attention to Mary Surratt. She still denied knowing the man who had appeared at her door on the night of her arrest, but she admitted that John Wilkes Booth had visited her house often. She said she "could not account for" Booth's decision to kill President Lincoln.

"I think no one could be more surprised than we were that he should be guilty of such an act," she said. "We often remarked that Mr. Booth was very clear of politics. He never mentioned anything of the kind, and it was a subject we never indulged in."

The detectives were hearing different stories from Lou Weichmann and tavern keeper John Lloyd. Lou described Mary Surratt's friendship with Booth and her trips to Surrattsville just before the assassination.

At first Lloyd denied knowing anything, but finally he said, "Oh, my God! If I should make a confession, they would murder me!"

"Who would murder you?" a soldier asked.

"These parties in the conspiracy," he said.

Soldiers put Lloyd in a guardhouse until he was ready to tell what had happened. After two days of sitting there, he was ready to talk.

He said Mary Surratt had come to the tavern just a few hours before the assassination. She had asked Lloyd to get the firearms ready because two men would come to pick them up at midnight.

After hearing this story, the detectives returned to Mrs. Surratt with more questions. Why had she gone to Surrattsville a few hours before the assassination? Why had she told Lloyd that the guns would soon be needed? Why had so many of the men in the assassination plot visited her house? How well did she know John Wilkes Booth? What did she know about the plot to kill the president?

Mary did not hesitate over her answers. She'd gone to Surrattsville, she said, because she'd gotten a letter about some debts. She denied telling John Lloyd anything about guns. The men in the assassination plot came to her house because she ran a boardinghouse that was open to the public. She thought Booth "was a handsome man and gentlemanly," and she did not know "he had the devil he certainly possessed in his heart."

She said she had never heard anything about a plot to kill President Lincoln. "Never in the world," she said, "if it was the last word I have ever to utter."

Anna also talked with the detectives—although she often said she did not know the answers to their questions.

The detectives began to sort out who belonged in prison and who didn't. It soon became clear that George Atzerodt, Lewis Powell, Sam Arnold, and Michael O'Laughlen were in serious trouble. So were Ned Spangler, a stagehand who had held Booth's horse for him in the alley behind Ford's Theatre, and Samuel Mudd, the Maryland doctor who had treated Booth's broken leg on the night of his escape. Newspapers reported that they were all chained in a boat at the Navy Yard, with hoods over their heads so they couldn't communicate with each other.

Newspapers also reported that John Wilkes Booth and David Herold had been found in Virginia, trapped in a barn. When Union soldiers set fire to the barn, Herold came running out, with his hands over his head.

Booth either killed himself or was shot by a soldier. Herold was brought back alone to Washington, where he was chained and hooded with the other male suspects.

After Booth was shot, soldiers dragged him from the fire they had started. *Courtesy Library of Congress.*

After a few days they all were transferred to the Old Arsenal Penitentiary, a military prison. There they awaited trial on charges of conspiring to assassinate the president of the United States.

Honora Fitzpatrick and Olivia Jenkins were released from the Carroll Annex, but Anna and her mother stayed on. They began to make friends with other prisoners.

Mary comforted one woman when she was separated from her husband. After that, the two women read the morning newspaper together. The papers often contained stories about Mary's involvement in President Lincoln's assassination. Some suggested she had been the mastermind who plotted the assassination.

One newspaper story said such nasty things about Mary Surratt that her new friends tried to hide the story from her. But she insisted on reading it. Then, Virginia Lomax later wrote, Mrs. Surratt was overcome by a "flush of womanly indignation. . . . After she had read it all, she laid the paper down and clasping her hands, raised her eyes to Heaven and said, 'I suppose I shall *have* to bear it.'"

Detectives kept questioning Mary about her son John. They knew by now of his role in the failed attempt to capture President Lincoln and were convinced that John Surratt also must have been part of the plot to murder the president. They wanted to arrest him, but didn't know where he was. They were sure his mother knew, though.

Mary Surratt insisted she did not know. She said she thought he had gone to Canada, but that was all she would say. Newspapers reported that prison officials offered Mrs. Surratt a deal: She could go free if she told them where her son had gone. Mary still insisted she did not know.

One Sunday evening two soldiers came to Mary's room and told her to put on her bonnet and cloak. Anna clung to her mother and begged for permission to go with her, but the soldiers said no. Mrs. Surratt had to go alone.

Mary hugged her friends and Anna. When she put her arms around Virginia Lomax, she pleaded, "Pray for me, pray for me!"

The soldiers took Mary down the stairs and out to a waiting carriage.

Anna sobbed, "Oh, Mother! Mother!" But the other prisoners were quiet. They thought Mary had been taken away for more questioning, and they waited for her return.

Some sat up all night, waiting, but Mary never returned. She had been taken to the Old Arsenal Penitentiary, along with the other prisoners accused of conspiring to kill Abraham Lincoln.

The Trial

The Old Arsenal Penitentiary was even bleaker than the Carroll Annex. The only furnishings in Mary Surratt's tiny cell were a thin pallet and a bucket. She slept on the pallet and used the bucket as a toilet.

She learned she was in a military prison because she was charged with conspiring to assassinate the president of the United States—which the government had decided was a war crime. Mrs. Surratt and seven other defendants would be tried as war criminals by a special military commission composed of nine Army officers.

The defendants would not have the right to testify on their own behalf or appeal their verdicts, but they did have the right to have attorneys represent them.

Prison cells at the Old Arsenal Penitentiary. *From the unpublished manuscript of Colonel Julian E. Raymond in the Joan L. Chaconas collection.*

Speaking through prison officials, Mary asked two well-known attorneys to defend her. They both refused. One later said he had wanted to defend her, but his father-in-law had objected because he didn't want the family's reputation soured by any association with the evil Mary Surratt.

A U.S. senator, Reverdy Johnson of Maryland, agreed to be her attorney. He said he did not know Mrs. Surratt, but "deemed it right" that she should have a lawyer. One of the military judges objected, recalling that Senator Johnson had criticized a loyalty oath required of Maryland citizens during the war.

Senator Johnson—who had worked with President Lincoln to keep Maryland in the Union during the war—became angry because he thought his own loyalty was being questioned. The judge withdrew his objection, but the senator was never much involved in Mary's case after that. He appeared only twice in court during the seven-week trial and left the day-to-day work of Mrs. Surratt's defense to two younger, inexperienced lawyers who had never before worked on a major case.

The young lawyers objected to a military trial. Because Mary Surratt was a private citizen, they said she was entitled to a trial with a jury made up of ordinary citizens.

The government said no. A president was commander in chief of military forces, and killing him during a war was a war crime. So the trial for his murder belonged in a military courtroom.

The trial was held in the Old Penitentiary building, just upstairs from Mary's cell. The courtroom was whitewashed, and gas lighting was installed for the occasion.

At first the trial was closed to the public, and even newspaper reporters weren't sure what was happening. But after newspapers complained about the secrecy, the government opened the trial to the public.

People came to gawk and hiss at the defendants, who sat in leg irons behind a railing in the back of the courtroom. The male

This drawing of the conspirators' trial shows Mrs. Surratt huddled in the right corner. Actually, she was separated from the other prisoners by a door. *Courtesy Surratt House Museum.*

defendants sat together, on one side of an iron door. Mary Surratt sat alone on the other side.

From the beginning, she was the defendant who drew the most attention. A reporter for *The Pittsburgh Daily Commercial* described people standing on tiptoe, straining to see Mary Surratt. The reporter recorded their comments: "Oh goodness, just look if she isn't pretending to be modest!" and, "She looks like a devil!" and, "Hasn't she a horrid face?" (Because Mary wore a heavy black veil, and kept a large fan between her face and the crowds, it's unlikely that anyone saw her face very well.)

As the trial wore on, though, it became obvious that Mary was ill. She leaned against a wall and groaned softly. One day she became so sick that guards had to remove her from the courtroom, and the trial had to be adjourned for the day. After that, she was moved from her tiny cell to a larger prison room, right next to the courtroom.

Prison officials didn't know what to do with a sick woman. So they let Anna, who had been released from the Carroll Annex, stay with her mother and take care of her.

Anna brought her mother's pillow from home so Mary could sleep more comfortably. Anna cared for her mother faithfully, but she was suffering, too. When she was called to testify at the trial, Anna answered questions calmly, but fainted afterward.

Almost four hundred witnesses testified at the trial. It soon became clear what most of the defendants had done. (Although Doctor Mudd claimed he hadn't recognized Booth when he fixed his broken leg, it was still clear that the doctor had fixed it.) It wasn't as clear what Mary Surratt had done.

Several people testified that she was a kind, Christian lady who never seemed interested in politics. Her old Surrattsville neighbors recalled how she had given food to Union soldiers without expecting payment. They described her poor eyesight,

Dr. Samuel Mudd later claimed he didn't recognize Booth when he fixed his leg—even though Booth had once spent the night at Dr. Mudd's house. *From the unpublished manuscript of Colonel Julian E. Raymond in the Joan L. Chaconas collection.*

Many people saw Mary Surratt as the center of the plot to kill Abraham
Lincoln. Others pictured here, from top left: John Wilkes Booth, Lewis
Powell (identified here as Payne), David Herold, Michael O'Laughlen,
John Surratt, Edward (Ned) Spangler, Samuel Arnold, and George
Atzerodt. Not Pictured: Dr. Samuel Mudd.

which might explain why she had not recognized Lewis Powell when he came to her house on the night of her arrest.

The most damaging evidence against Mary Surratt came from her former boarder, Lou Weichmann, and tavern keeper John Lloyd. Lou described her friendship with Booth—how the two of them would sometimes talk privately for two or three hours at a time. He also described the two trips she made to Surrattsville the week before the assassination.

Lloyd described how John Surratt had hidden guns—sometimes called "shooting irons"—at the tavern he rented from Mary Surratt. A few hours before the assassination, Lloyd said, Mrs. Surratt "told me to have those shooting irons ready that night—there would be some parties call for them." Prosecutors pointed to this as proof that Mary Surratt had known about the plans to kill President Lincoln.

Some people even thought Mary Surratt had made the plans herself—and Booth was just following her instructions when he shot the president. Andrew Johnson, who became president after Abraham Lincoln's death, said Mrs. Surratt "kept the nest that hatched the egg" of the assassination.

Others were just as sure that Mary was completely innocent. They said both Lou Weichmann and John Lloyd testified against her because they were afraid that if they didn't, they would become suspects themselves.

Some people thought the government was using Mrs. Surratt's trial to lure her son John out of hiding. John Surratt remained a prime suspect in the assassination plot, but no one knew where he was. Investigators hoped he would become so worried about his mother that he would return to Washington and turn himself in.

But John Surratt did not return, and the trial ended on June 28, 1865.

Mercy!

*I*t took the military judges just one day to decide on Mary Surratt's guilt. They found her, Lewis Powell, David Herold, and George Atzerodt guilty of conspiring to kill the president of the United States. All four were sentenced to death.

The judges took a little longer reaching a decision about Dr. Mudd. Four of the nine judges wanted to sentence him to death, but in the end, they decided to send him to prison for the rest of his life. They also sentenced Samuel Arnold and Michael O'Laughlen to life in prison. Ned Spangler was sentenced to six years in prison, as punishment for holding Booth's horse while the actor went inside Ford's Theatre.

On July 5, 1865, Judge Advocate General Joseph Holt took papers to President Andrew Johnson announcing the court's decisions. The papers included a separate petition, signed by five of the nine military judges, recommending that President Johnson change Mary Surratt's sentence to life imprisonment. The federal government had never hanged a woman before, and the judges said they wanted to spare Mrs. Surratt "in consideration of her sex and age." (She was forty-two.)

Their petition didn't change anything. President Johnson signed the paper ordering the execution of Mary Surratt, along with Powell, Herold, and Atzerodt.

The president later claimed he never saw the petition recommending mercy for Mrs. Surratt. Judge Holt insisted he had shown the petition to the president. They disagreed about this for the rest of their lives.

Mary Surratt was still sick from her months in prison when she learned on the afternoon of July 6 that she would be hanged the very next day. At first she couldn't believe it.

"I had no hand in the murder of the president," she said softly. Then she began to cry. She called for Anna, her priests, and a few friends.

One of the priests, Father Jacob Ambrose Walter, heard Mary's confession—a sacrament where Roman Catholics confess their sins to a priest. Then Father Walter and Anna raced to the White House. President Johnson was the only one who could save Mary now, and surely he would be moved by the sight of the weeping daughter and a holy priest.

At the White House gate, Anna and Father Walter met a former congressman who told them he was "on the same errand of mercy. The president must not allow this woman to be hanged!"

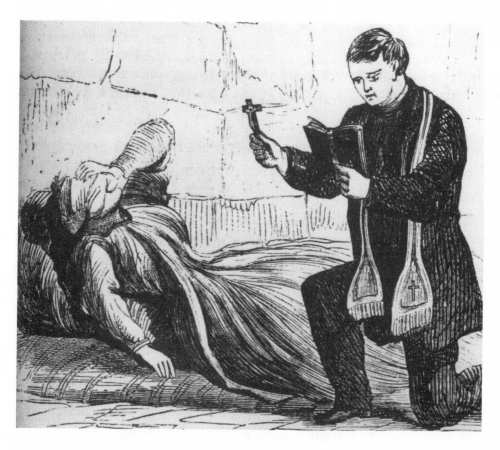

This illustration in the *National Police Gazette* showed Mary Surratt receiving the last sacraments of the Catholic Church. *Courtesy Surratt House Museum.*

Others rushed to the White House to beg for Mary Surratt's life. Even the superintendent of the Old Capitol Prison came as soon as he heard that Mary had been sentenced to death.

President Johnson refused, through his aides, to speak with Anna, the priest, the congressman, or anyone else about Mary Surratt. The aides told Anna to see Judge Holt, the man who had brought the military commission's papers to the president. But Judge Holt said he could not help.

When Mary Surratt's lawyers heard about her sentence, they began looking for ways to save her. They decided to present a writ of habeas corpus, a petition asking for a hearing, to another court. Because Mary was a private citizen in Washington, D.C., her lawyers still claimed she had a right to a civil trial in Washington—which made her military trial illegal, they said.

The lawyers finished writing the petition that night and delivered it to the home of a Washington judge in the wee hours of the morning. A few hours later, the judge received a letter from President Johnson, saying he had suspended habeas corpus in this case. The judge thought the president's decision settled the matter and refused to grant Mrs. Surratt a hearing.

Anna returned to the White House to plead for her mother's life. President Johnson still refused to see her. The only person who managed to see the president about Mary Surratt was Adele Douglas, the widow of former presidential candidate Stephen A. Douglas. President Johnson greeted Mrs. Douglas warmly, but when he realized why she had come, he turned her away, too.

President Andrew Johnson. *Courtesy Andrew Johnson National Historic Site, Greeneville, Tennessee.*

Anna threw herself, sobbing, on the marble steps at the White House. Finally a friend pulled her away, saying she should return to the prison if she wanted to see her mother before she died.

Even in the last minutes of Mary Surratt's life, many people expected President Johnson to change her sentence to life in

Moments before their deaths, from left to right, Mary Surratt (seated and shaded by umbrellas), Lewis Powell (hooded), David Herold, and George Atzerodt. *From the Joan L. Chaconas collection.*

prison. They were sure the death sentence was one last attempt to bring John Surratt out of hiding. Surely John wouldn't let his mother hang! And surely the president would stop—or at least delay—her hanging if John appeared.

With that in mind, the commander of the military prison stationed soldiers along the route to the White House. If the president changed Mrs. Surratt's sentence, the soldiers could quickly relay the message back to the prison.

But John Surratt did not appear, and the president did not change the sentence. So shortly after one o'clock, Mary Surratt was led to the gallows.

It was a blistering hot day, and Mrs. Surratt was still sick, so soldiers half-carried her up the thirteen steps to a platform with four nooses. She was helped to a chair, where a soldier held an umbrella over her head to protect her from the sun's glare. She moaned when she saw the noose hanging in front of her, so a priest stepped in front of it to block her view.

Lewis Powell, David Herold, and George Atzerodt stood—without umbrellas—to face their own nooses.

Powell looked over at Mary Surratt and said, "She does not deserve to die with the rest of us."

But her arms and legs were bound and the noose was slipped over her head. Watching from the prison's second-story window, Anna Surratt fainted. When she regained consciousness, her mother was dead.

John

*F*or almost two years, the United States government searched for John Surratt. Where was he, and why hadn't he returned to save his mother?

On the night of the assassination, John had been in Elmira, New York, delivering yet another message for the Confederates. When he saw a newspaper story that connected him with the assassination plot, he decided to leave the country.

He took a train to Canada, where friends hid him for several months. They evidently also hid newspapers because he later said he did not know how serious his mother's plight was until the day she was hanged.

Then John fled to Europe, where he served in the papal guard at the Vatican, headquarters of the Roman Catholic church. A

John Surratt as a papal guard. *Courtesy Surratt House Museum.*

Maryland man recognized John Surratt at the Vatican and reported him to authorities, who arrested John and placed him in a cell.

One morning he asked to use the latrine—an outside toilet—after breakfast. While guards waited for him, he jumped over a wall to rocks 30 feet below. Even though he was injured, he made his way to Naples, Italy, where he boarded a ship bound for Alexandria, Egypt.

When the ship docked, Egyptian soldiers rushed on board and took John Surratt into custody. He was brought back to Washington—under tight security—and held in the Old Capitol Prison while he awaited trial in 1867 on charges of conspiring to murder Abraham Lincoln.

By then, so many people had criticized his mother's military trial that John Surratt was granted a civil trial with a jury made up of ordinary citizens.

The trial lasted sixty-one days and ended in a hung jury. The jurors simply couldn't agree about whether he was guilty of plotting to kill the president. Jurors with Northern sympathies said he was guilty, and jurors with Southern sympathies said he was not guilty.

With a split like that, the prosecutors decided the country was still too divided to judge John Surratt fairly. So they charged him with something clearer: treason, or attempting to overthrow the United States government. He had, after all, carried messages for the Confederate government.

As he grew older, John Surratt continued to defend his mother's innocence. *Courtesy Surratt House Museum.*

But a judge pointed out that the statute of limitations on treason—that is, the amount of time the law allowed for the government to file charges of treason against a citizen—had run out. So John Surratt became a free man on November 5, 1868.

For the rest of their lives, he and Anna maintained that their mother was innocent.

Was she?

For years, Americans have argued about Mary Surratt's role in the death of President Lincoln. Was she simply a Maryland mother who did a few favors for a friend? Or was she, as Judge Holt once claimed, "the master spirit" among those who plotted to kill the president?

She obviously knew all of the conspirators. They visited her house often, and several spent the night. She was a friend of John Wilkes Booth, often talking privately with him and doing special favors for him. She took his field glasses to the Surrattsville tavern on the day of the assassination, and, according to the tavern keeper, she told him to get the guns and supplies ready because they would be needed that night.

But did she know what she was doing? Did she say and do these things because she thought she was doing a few favors and passing along a few messages for a friend? Or did she say and do these things because she was part of the plot to kill Abraham Lincoln?

What do *you* think?

Epilogue

John Wilkes Booth died on a Virginia farm on April 27, 1865. Mary Surratt, Lewis Powell, George Atzerodt, and David Herold were hanged on July 7 of that year for their parts in the assassination of Abraham Lincoln.

What became of the others involved in the mystery of Mary Surratt?

Samuel Arnold—Originally sentenced to life in prison for his part in the attempted kidnapping of President Lincoln, Arnold was released in 1869 after receiving a presidential pardon from Andrew Johnson. He later lived alone on his Maryland farm and died of pulmonary tuberculosis in 1906 at the age of seventy-two.

President Andrew Johnson—The former vice president had a rocky presidency in the years after the Civil War. Congress never liked him, and the House of Representatives voted to impeach him in 1868. Mary Surratt's daughter, Anna, was one of those who testified during his trial in the Senate. He escaped removal from office by one vote in 1869 and did not run for the presidency the following year. Tennessee sent him back to Washington as a U.S. senator in 1874, but he died the following year after a paralytic stroke.

John Lloyd—Unable to stay in Surrattsville after his testimony led to Mary Surratt's conviction and execution, he returned to Washington, D.C., where he worked as a bricklayer. He died in a fall at a construction site in 1892 at the age of sixty-eight.

Dr. Samuel Mudd—Originally sentenced to life in prison for his part in helping Booth escape, he was pardoned in 1869 after he took care of prisoners and guards during an outbreak of yellow fever at the prison in Dry Tortugas, Florida. He returned home and resumed his medical practice near Waldorf, Maryland. He died of pneumonia in 1883 at the age of forty-nine. His children, grandchildren, and great-grandchildren fought to clear his name until 2003 when the U.S. Supreme Court refused to hear their case.

Michael O'Laughlen—Sentenced to life in prison, he died in 1867 during the yellow fever epidemic at the prison on Dry Tortugas. He was twenty-eight.

Edman (Ned) Spangler—Sentenced to six years in prison for his part in helping Booth escape, he was released after receiving a presidential pardon in 1869. He lived on Dr. Mudd's farm until his death in 1875 at the age of forty-nine.

Anna Surratt—She lived with friends until 1869 when she married a chemist, William Tonry, who lost his government job after he married the daughter of the infamous Mary Surratt. They moved to Baltimore, where they raised four children. Anna died in 1904 at the age of sixty-one. Some people in Washington claim they have seen her ghost, knocking on the White House door and begging for her mother's life.

Isaac Surratt—Serving in the Confederate Army in Texas at the time of his mother's trial and execution, Mary Surratt's oldest son did not hear of her death for several months. He later returned to Baltimore and worked for a steamship company until his death in 1907 at the age of sixty-one.

John Surratt—After his release from prison in 1868, he traveled across the United States, giving speeches about his life. Later, he married, had a family, and became auditor and treasurer of the Baltimore steamship company where his brother worked. He died of pneumonia in 1916 at the age of seventy-two.

Louis Weichmann—After the trial, he went back to working for the federal government. He stayed in Washington until the 1880s when he returned to his home state of Indiana, where he started a business college. Because so many people criticized him for testifying against Mary Surratt, he wrote a book explaining his role, but it was not published until 1975—more than seventy years after his death in 1902 at the age of fifty-nine.

If you want to learn more. . . .

The best place to learn about Mary Surratt is at the Surratt House Museum in Clinton, Maryland. (Surrattsville changed its name to Clinton after the Lincoln assassination.) Operated by the Surratt Society, the house and tavern are open to visitors, and they look much the same as they did when Mary and her family lived there. You can visit the museum, ask questions of the guides, and browse through thousands of books and research files at the museum's James O. Hall Research Center.

While you're in the area, you can also visit Dr. Samuel A. Mudd's farmhouse near Waldorf, Maryland, and the Ford's Theatre and The House Where Lincoln Died, both in the 500 block of Tenth Street Northwest in Washington, D.C. Mary

Surratt's old boardinghouse still stands on H Street in Washington, but it is now a Chinese restaurant.

You don't have to travel to Washington or Maryland to learn more about the Lincoln assassination. The Surratt Society has an informative Web site at http://www.surratt.org. If you visit a library with newspapers (on microfilm) dating back to 1865, you can read old news stories about the Lincoln assassination and the trial of the conspirators.

You can also find information in the many books that have been written about the Lincoln assassination. One of the most fascinating is *Lincoln's Assassins: Their Trial and Execution,* by James L. Swanson and Daniel R. Weinberg. It is filled with photographs and drawings related to the Lincoln assassination. *Mary Surratt: An American Tragedy,* by Elizabeth Steger Trindall, focuses on Mary and her family. *The President Has Been Shot: True Stories of the Attacks on Ten U.S. Presidents,* by Rebecca C. Jones, describes the Lincoln assassination along with the attempts on other presidents' lives.

Two of the men involved in the Lincoln assassination investigation wrote memoirs that are still available. Samuel Arnold, who was imprisoned for his part in the attempt to capture President Lincoln, wrote *Memoirs of a Lincoln Conspirator,* edited by Michael W. Kauffman. Louis Weichmann, John Surratt's best friend and a boarder at the house on H Street, wrote *A True History of the Assassination of Abraham Lincoln and of the Conspiracy of 1865,* edited by Floyd E. Risvold.

In case you're wondering, Sam Arnold's book says Mary Surratt was innocent, and Lou Weichmann's says she was guilty.

Acknowledgments

A lot of people helped me untangle Mary Surratt's story. I am most grateful to James O. Hall, one of the foremost experts on the Abraham Lincoln assassination. He welcomed me into his home and made available his private files. He also contributed much of the research material that's available at the Surratt House Museum in Clinton, Maryland. (No wonder the museum's new library has been named the James O. Hall Research Center.) He reviewed this book for accuracy and made many valuable suggestions. Any errors that remain are my own.

The entire staff at the Surratt House Museum was helpful. Museum director Laurie Verge runs a premiere (and accessible) research organization. Joan Chaconas welcomed every question and spent hours tracking down photographs. Research librarian

Chris Witherspoon guided me through resources, and Margery Patten became a good friend and ally.

Most of the photographs and drawings in this book were originally published in the 1860s, at the time of the Lincoln assassination. (The only exceptions are the map on page 11 and the photograph of John Surratt on page 81.) Most came from the Surratt House Museum, Joan Chaconas's private collection, and the Library of Congress, but I also want to thank Elaine Clark of the Andrew Johnson National Historic Site in Greeneville, Tennessee, and Cindy VanHorn of The Lincoln Museum in Fort Wayne, Indiana.

I am also grateful to Michael Kauffman, who leads semiannual tours of the Booth escape route; to media specialist Jan Smith, who offered advice on making Mary Surratt's story accessible to young readers; and to the late Mike Maione, a Lincoln assassination expert at Ford's Theatre, who shared his knowledge, resources, and theories.

Finally, I want to thank my husband, Chris Jones, for cheerfully enduring this project.

Index